How Sammy Sees the World

How Sammy Sees the World

Written by Lily Love Loudon (at age 10)

Edited by Dr. Gina Loudon **Illustrated by Mike Sofka**

BEYOND WORDS
Portland, Oregon

BEYOND WORDS

1750 S.W. Skyline Blvd., Suite 20
Portland, Oregon 97221-2543
503–531–8700/503–531–8773 fax
www.beyondword.com

This first Beyond Words hardcover edition March 2026

Editor: Michele Ashtiani Cohn
Design: Mike Sofka

The text of this book was set in Adobe Caslon Pro and Orange Juice Regular.
The illustrations for this book were rendered in Procreate.

Beyond Words Publishing is an imprint of Simon & Schuster, LLC,
and the Beyond Words logo is a registered trademark of Beyond Words Publishing, Inc.

For more information about special discounts for bulk purchases,
please contact Beyond Words Special Sales at 503–531–8700 or specialsales@beyondword.com.

Manufactured in the United States of America

10 9 8 7 6 5 4 3 2 1

ISBN 978-1-58270-974-1 (hardcover)
ISBN 978-1-58270-975-8 (ebook)

The corporate mission of Beyond Words Publishing, Inc.: *Inspire to Integrity*

Dedicated to my amazing brother Sam,
to my parents who made it a mission to save him,
and to all the families out there who choose life! *L'chaim!*

Sammy sees the world in quite a different way.

Yes, he loves to sing, dance, laugh, and play!

Like many others, he lives and
loves each day!

But Sammy sees the world...

In quite a different way.
For example:

People see Santa Claus,
Sammy sees a friend!

People play a song once,
Sammy says again!

People see a tree, Sammy
sees a playground!

People follow directions,
Sammy wanders around!

People see an ocean,
Sammy sees a waterpark!

Sammy hears a dog sing
when people hear it bark.

People see a blanket...

Sammy sees a fort!

Sammy warms your heart
when people make it hurt.

Sammy was adopted, his
love needed to be spread.

People see a birth mom,
Sammy sees a friend instead.

People see his parents, not related to him by blood.

But Sammy knows they chose him with every bit of their love.

Sammy can do things
just like you and me...

But Sammy has something extra,
a little more special you see.

Sammy loves to sing,
dance, laugh, and play.

Yes, Sammy sees the world
in quite a different way!

Author's Note

When I was about 10 years old, I wrote this book for my brother Samuel. It was just meant to be a little gift for him to read at bedtime, until my mother discovered it about a decade later and suggested we publish it, so here we are!

Even at a young age, I knew Sammy was different from other kids. He has Down Syndrome, but I didn't know what that was. People just said "different" or "special" to explain his condition when our family adopted him as a baby. My innocent mind thought that was, to some degree, a bad thing.

As he grew, I noticed he is indeed different and special, but not how my little brain first thought. He doesn't need extra help—*we* do. And that's why God created people like Sammy.

I wrote this book to explain how Sammy is different in a way kids like me could understand.

He finds beauty in the ugly, happy in the sad, extraordinary in the ordinary. He is a little bubble of all the good things in the world and further proof that God makes *no* mistakes.

He may seem lesser to people, both adults and children, who don't understand, but that's part of what makes him so incredible. Though he may not make sense of things the same way others do, he approaches life in ways most people could never begin to understand.

We hope this book blesses your family and friends and that maybe someone out there is inspired to give a little guy like my brother Sammy a forever family.

—Lily Love Loudon

About the Author

Photo Courtesy of Author

Elizabeth Love Loudon, known as Lily after Luke 12:27 ("Consider the lilies how they grow: they toil not, they spin not; and yet I say unto you, that Solomon in all his glory was not arrayed like one of these"), was born and raised in the Christian faith along with her four siblings. She wrote this book when she was 10 years old for her adopted brother, Samuel, who has Down Syndrome.

About the Editor

Photo Courtesy of Author

Dr. Gina Loudon holds two master's degrees and a PhD, all with top honors. A bestselling author and national news commentator (FOX News, FOX Business, CNN, and others), Dr. Gina has anchored on Newsmax and Real America's Voice, hosting Dr. Gina Prime Time and American Sunrise. She was a national delegate for President Trump to the 2016 RNC. She cochaired Women for Trump and is a long-time advisor to him. She contributes to outlets like Breitbart and FOXNEWS.com. Dr. Gina's recent awards include the Moms for America Mothers of Influence Award, the Conservative Women's Voices Preserving Freedom Award, and the Lee Greenwood Patriot Award. She loves philanthropy and water sports and is a homeschool mom to her five children, one by the blessing of adoption who has Down Syndrome.

About the Illustrator

Photo by Stephanie Sofka

Mike Sofka is an illustrator and designer who contributed to several *VeggieTales* productions, including *The League of Incredible Vegetables* (2012) and *The Penniless Princess* (2012). His work encompassed both visual design and voice acting roles. Beyond VeggieTales, Sofka has collaborated with organizations such as the Walt Disney Company. He currently operates his own illustration and design business.

Purchase Sammy's Stuff

and support They All Have Names

People with Down Syndrome have one extra chromosome. Today, 80% of babies with Down Syndrome are aborted, while 300 families sit waiting to adopt them. Our family was one of those, and we waited 10 years to adopt Sammy.

We want to help other families give babies like Sammy their forever homes. If you do too, please purchase Sammy's Stuff and support They All Have Names.

—Dr. Gina Loudon

SammysSocks.com

TheyAllHaveNames.com